RHYMING REVELATION

RHYMING REVELATION

Maxine Lantz

WESTBOW
PRESS
A DIVISION OF THOMAS NELSON

WestBow Press books may be ordered through booksellers or by contacting:

WestBow Press
A Division of Thomas Nelson
1663 Liberty Drive
Bloomington, IN 47403
www.westbowpress.com
1-(866) 928-1240

ISBN: 978-1-4497-5562-1 (e)
ISBN: 978-1-4497-5561-4 (sc)

Library of Congress Control Number: 2012910284

Printed in the United States of America

WestBow Press rev. date: 09/21/2012

AUTHOR'S FOREWORD

I have called this booklet of poetry "Rhyming Revelation" because God gave me the words to write. I am merely God's typist. The central heart on the front cover symbolizes God's great love for me that has given me other loves in my life (all the smaller hearts).

I hope that these poems will give you some insight into what I believe is the true character of God and his son, Jesus Christ. I thank God for saving me, and I look forward to spending eternity with God and Jesus Christ.

I pray that these poems will edify the reader, and that those who know Christ as Saviour will be encouraged to continue their walk with him. For the reader that does not yet know Christ in this personal way, I pray that these words will lead you to the point in your life where you will accept Christ as your personal Saviour.

I would also like to take this opportunity to thank the keepers of my words. Each poem I write gets sent to my sister (Lynda Taylor), my husband Jim, my pastor and his wife (John & Cheryl Scorgie, who are also dear friends), and to another two dear friends (Carrol Ross & Joyce Lindsay). They are my biggest supporters, and I thank them for their love, loyalty and faithfulness.

Thank-you,
Maxine Lantz

Other Books By This Author:

Love On The Wing

Flights Of Fancy

Covenant Of Care

Basking In The Son-Shine

Abundant Life

CONTENTS

A CHANGED SONG

I sang a song of doubt and fears;
Each note was filled with countless tears.
Each chord resounded, full of pain;
Each beat was full of strife and strain.

Tune and words could not make rhyme;
I was sad and lonely all the time.
I had no friend on which to lean.
My life felt sullied, all unclean.

But in all those uncertain days
I then remembered all the ways
When you had brought me through the same.
I only need to call your name.

My song now echoes with new life;
No longer is there strain and strife.
No longer is there doubt and pain;
My life, my heart, feels new again.

I have a friend who'll never leave.
The worry is replaced with peace.
I have no need to sing sad songs
For now, my heart to Christ belongs.

A MOTHER, BY GOD

I cannot be the mother
That God wants me to be
Without His loving guidance
That each new day I see.

I cannot be the victor
In the race I run each day
Unless I near the throne of grace,
Fall on my knees and pray.

I cannot teach my children
What they must know to live
Until I do experience
The loving grace God gives.

I cannot nurture all the ones
That God gave me to love
Without the patient teaching
From my Father up above.

I cannot wait to tell you –
And this truth is like no other –
Without the Father in my heart,
I'd never be God's kind of mother.

A mom who loves those in her home,
A mom who lives in peace,
A mom whose focus on her God
Makes happiness increase.

A mom who'd gladly give her life
For those she loves the most,
For Christ is her example –
He didn't count the cost.

A mom whose joy is in the Lord,
Who tells her kids the news
That Jesus died for all their sin
And they must someday choose

To follow Christ, pick up His cross
And live for Him each day.
Her children learn this every day
As she reads God's word and prays.

And when she walks this earth no more
And from earthly strife is freed,
God will welcome her and say, "Well done!
You left a Christian legacy."

A NEW YEAR

I'm looking at a new year, Lord, -
A book all clean and new.
I don't know what will happen;
I don't know what I'll do.

I'll write upon each new page
A tale of wrong or right.
Each word will be an action
Done in darkness or in light.

Each chapter will hold the story
Of righteousness or sin.
Will I stand firm in the faith of Christ
Or let the Temptor win?

I do not know the ending
Nor how long the book will be.
I only know that, as you've said,
You won't depart from me.

Together we will journey
As I fill each new day's lines,
And when the book's completed
It'll be a MASTER-piece design.

ALL ABOARD!

The holy Train Conductor
Will shout out "All aboard!".
Then folks from all around the earth
Will listen to his words.
They'll climb each step with gratitude,
With loving and with hope.
In any situation, with Him,
They know they'll cope.

They'll leave behind their bags of fear,
Their suitcases of grief.
They'll leave them on the platform
And move on with great relief.
There'll be piles of dread and sorrow
And mounds of past misdeeds.
They'll all be left behind by folks
When the Train Conductor leads.

They'll fellowship with others
Who have also joined the train.
The love that they experience
Will wipe away their pain.
They'll know the future holds no fear,
And that death will bring an end.
But they know the Train Conductor knows
What's coming 'round the bend.

Then the Train Conductor hollers
To the Engineer in red
"All these folks have their tickets.
Let's go! Full speed ahead!"
And the train of truth will clatter,
'Round the bend and down the shore
Till the train will cross the silver sea,
And stop at Heaven's door.

When the passengers step off the train,
And enter Heaven's gate,
Their songs of praise will multiply,
Their joy will be so great.
They'll thank the Train Conductor
For all that he has done
And thank the Engineer as well
For his help on their lives' run.

So, those of you who have not heard
The call of "All Aboard"
Should think just what your life will be
Without our Savior Lord.
How will you get to Heaven's gate,
If the Train you did not ride,
And you never heard the Conductor's call,
And never went inside?

ALL-SUFFICIENT GRACE

But he said to me, "My grace is sufficient for you,
for my power is made perfect in weakness."

2 Corinthians 12:9 NIV

It matters not the circumstance;
It matters not the place.
I know the Father's watching
And will cover me in grace.

When I am at my weakest,
My God does me amaze
And fortifies me with His power
And His amazing grace.

No matter what I've said or done,
When I seek my Father's face,
My God's forgiveness will be shown
And He'll shower me with grace.

The shower won't a trickle be;
It won't be just a trace.
I'll know God's mercy and I'll be
Washed in a flood of grace.

This grace is all-sufficient;
This grace suits every case.
I know my life's dependent on
My God's amazing grace.

It can't be bought or bartered;
No gold could take its place.
But the Father gives me freely
Of His all-sufficient grace.

BE LIKE JESUS

Your attitude should be the same as that of Christ Jesus: Who, being in very nature God, did not consider equality with God something to be grasped, but made himself nothing, taking the very nature of a servant, being made in human likeness. And being found in appearance as a man, he humbled himself and became obedient to death— even death on a cross!

Philippians 2:5-8 NIV

Your attitude should be the same
As Jesus Christ, the King.
In all your actions and your thoughts,
Be like Him in all things.
He did not want equality,
Though God he was in truth,
He took on human likeness,
And a servant's nature, too.
And being found just as a man,
He showed humility
And went obedient to the cross
To save us, you and me.
He knew the end that waited there,
A death of shame and pain,
But He went willingly to His death
To save us from sin's stain.
As He hung upon that cruel cross,
His pain was clear to see,
But He endured that torturous death
To redeem sinful me.
The weight of all the world's sin
Was placed on Him that day.
What anguish did He suffer when
God turned his face away?
For God could not regard the sin
His son bore for us all.
He never used the heavenly hordes
Of angels He could call.

He never used His heavenly might,
His truly divine power.
For He looked forward, the third day,
To His resurrection hour.
When bursting forth, in glory bright,
He conquered death's cold grave
And He fulfilled His Father's plan
For all mankind to be saved.
The plan that tells us those who call
On God with sorrowed heart
Will gain abundant life on earth
With grace God will impart.
His love and mercy will be theirs
For all their time on earth
And when in heaven with the Lord,
Their lives will find their worth.

BE STRONG AND COURAGEOUS

Have I not commanded you? Be strong and courageous.
Do not be terrified; do not be discouraged, for the
LORD your God will be with you wherever you go.

Joshua 1:9 NIV

Be strong and courageous.
Don't let fear take the reins.
Believe that God's mercy
Will always remain.

For fear is the victor
When you go it alone,
But with God beside you
Your strength will be shown.

And don't be discouraged
For you rest in His care.
God's love and protection
Will always be there.

There is no location
Where God will not be.
Just cry to Jehovah
And His grace you will see.

When trials all surround you
And your world is all wrong,
Remember God's great love
And be courageous and strong.

BY NO OTHER NAME

*Salvation is found in no one else, for there
is no other name under heaven given to
men by which we must be saved.*

By no other name is salvation acquired.
By no other name are we cleansed from our sins
By no other name are heaven's gates opened
So that we may enter within.

By no other name can we claim all His power.
By no other name do we find ourselves healed.
By no other name do the demons start running
For they know that their destiny's sealed.

By no other name are we rescued from Satan.
By no other name are we loosed from his snare.
By no other name is the Temptor defeated
For we rest in Christ's loving care.

By no other name do we have quiet assurance.
By no other name we experience peace.
By no other name do we call out in trouble
For we know that His love won't cease.

CALVARY

I heard your quiet whispers, Lord,
But I never chose to heed.
You spoke of sin that led to death,
But I thought I had no need.
The truth was all around me,
And yet I could not see
Till you called me up to Calvary
On my knees.

My life was filled with only pleasure,
Not thinking of hell's flames.
Not thinking of my own Creator,
Not calling on His name.
Not thinking of the end of life,
Until the hour I came
And I heard you call from Calvary,
Without blame.

You spoke no words of condemnation,
No words fell on my ears.
You reached out with your nail-pierced hands,
And wiped away my tears.
Within my soul, I realized
That I had no cause to fear.
The love that was shown at Calvary
Made it clear.

I never need to fear life's end,
For the great prize lies beyond.
A future filled with glory
Where the other saints have gone.
A future filled with praising God
For the love that He has shown.
Due to the words at Calvary, when Christ said
"It is done."

COME TO THE CROSS

Come to the cross, yes, come to the cross
With all of your sorrows and care.
Come to the cross, the blood splattered cross,
And the Savior will meet with you there.

Come to the cross, yes, come to the cross
Do not wait for another day.
Come to the cross, the redemptive cross,
And the Savior will show you the way.

Come to the cross, yes, come to the cross,
Your fears will be replaced with peace.
Come to the cross, the glorious cross,
For a deep love that will never cease.

Come to the cross, yes, come to the cross
Your life will be forever changed.
Come to the cross, the salvation cross,
Just call on our dear Savior's name.

Come to the cross, yes, come to the cross
You don't have to be perfect, my friend.
Come to the cross, the old rugged cross,
You'll find mercy and grace without end.

Come to the cross, yes, come to the cross
Just confess your sins to the Lord.
Come to the cross, the soul-cleansing cross,
You'll find comfort in his Holy Word.

Just come to the cross with repentant heart
Forgiveness will be what you receive
And God's perfect peace, His mercy and grace
Will be offered, if you'll only believe.

CONTINUE TO LIVE IN CHRIST JESUS

*So then, just as you received Christ Jesus as
Lord, continue to live in him, rooted and built
up in him, strengthened in the faith as you were
taught, and overflowing with thankfulness.*

Colossians 2:6-7 NIV

Continue to live in Christ Jesus, the Lord
For you received Him as Savior and King.
Stay rooted firmly in His holy word
And, in Him, you can achieve all things.
Be built up in Him and rest in His care,
With faith strengthened as you were taught.
And never forget Christ's sacrifice made
So your soul, with His blood, could be bought.
Be forever thankful in all circumstance
For in each case, this thought is true -
That if God brings you to a temptation or trial,
Then God will deliver you through.
Be bold to proclaim to all those who are lost
That the Christ that you love and adore
Can be theirs if they'll yield up their repentant heart
And abide in His love evermore.
For narrow's the gateway, and narrow the path
That leads up to glory on high.
But the souls that will walk and enter the gate
Will rejoice when they hear Jesus' cry,
"My Child, I'm so glad that you've finally come home.
I've prepared a mansion and crown.
I've waited forever to talk face-to-face
Come, let's walk over heaven's gold ground."

COUNT ME WORTHY

The man was selected
From out of the crowd
To carry the cross for my Lord.
If he had refused,
He knew for a fact
That he'd die at the end of a sword.

He struggled to stand up
And bear that great load.
The sweat fell in drops from his brow.
He staggered and watched
As Christ's blood ran pure red
From the scourging and cruel thorny crown.

When he had be given
His freedom again,
I wonder what went through his mind.
Was he glad that the cross
Was a burden no more?
Or did he, in his labour, Christ find.

So, Lord, let me never
Be ashamed of your name.
May I not find myself at a loss
To explain all the work
That you've done in my life.
Lord, count me worthy to carry your cross.

CUPPED AND COVERED

I give them eternal life, and they shall never perish; no one can snatch them out of my hand. My Father, who has given them to me, is greater than all; no one can snatch them out of my Father's hand. I and the Father are one.

John 10:28-30 NIV

I'm standing in the hollow
Of Christ, My Savior's hand
His father's hands are o'er me,
And now I understand
That no power, principality
Or any mortal man
Can take me from the loving place
Where now I firmly stand.
I'm standing in the hollow,
And know that heaven's mine.
I only have to listen
And heed God's word divine.
I'll live a life abundant here on Earth
And when it's time
I'll sit beside the Bridegroom
And at His feast I'll dine.
The Father gave me to Him.
I claim Him as my King.
With Jesus Christ beside me,
I need no other thing.
I'll honor Son and Father,
And to them praises sing,
And to my life, each day I live,
Unchanging love they'll bring.
And if you ask, with contrite heart,
They'll do the same for you.
Repent, admit that you have sinned.
That's all you have to do.

Eternal life with God and Christ,
What else would someone choose?
Then peace and joy, when found in Christ,
Is something you can't lose.

DANCE OF LIFE

In the crazy dance of life, Lord,
You always hold my hand.
And when I spin a bit too much,
Your hand helps me to stand.
And when the dance gets out of hand,
Then this thought comforts much
That no matter what the speed of life,
I never lose your touch.

It doesn't matter if the world
Is spinning round and round
I know I've just to reach out, Lord,
And your loving hand is found.
We'll spin through life, Lord, hand in hand
And never will I fear
For my hand in yours is all I need.
I'll always need you near!

And when the pace of life slows down,
We waltz along life's trail
And view the world and what you've made.
Our joy will never fail.
We dance together, hand in hand,
To the music you have wrought
In my life since to you, my Lord,
My sin-stained heart I brought.

I know that you will never take
Your hand from within mine
And we'll dance the stately dance of life,
To music so divine.
And I know that for eternity I'll try,
If given half a chance,
To thank you, Lord, for holding me
In the moments of life's dance.

DROSS TO GLORY

I packed up all my guilt and sin.
It took me quite a while.
My will and disobedience
Were then added to the pile.
I found some space for fear and doubt.
The box was filled with dross.
I took them all to Jesus Christ
As He hung upon the cross.

I laid them at the Savior's feet
And as my tears were streaming down,
A drop of Christ's own crimson blood
Fell from His thorny crown.
It fell upon my shame-bowed head,
A single drop of red.
I felt it sink down deep within
As He hung there in my stead.

My soul was cleansed of all its sin.
I was a creature new.
For Christ's red blood, His sacrifice,
My life it there renewed.
He took my sin and all the rest
And gave me second birth.
His blood gave royal status
And gave my life great worth.

What I gave up was nothing -
A life of shame and sin.
But what I gained in Jesus Christ
I scarce can take it in.
I gained a peace from heaven,
And joy that knows no end,
A love with no conditions,
And I gained Jesus as my friend.

GAIN IN LOSS

When we walk up in heaven
As we sing and praise the King.
We'll notice some things missing,
But they won't be worth a thing.

We won't see any crying,
No tears and no more pain.
No night, no death, nor sorrow,
Will fill our days again.

No hunger or defilement,
No sorrow or no curse,
And we'll have living water
To satisfy our thirst.

No selfishness will crowd out
Our worship of our God.
No racism or worries
Will mar the world we trod.

Disease won't gain a foothold
To take away our peace.
The peace that we experience
Will never, ever cease.

Misunderstandings won't take place
No quarrels mar the joy
Of the time we spend with Jesus.
It's the end of Satan's ploys.

We never will feel insecure
For we will know the love
Of He who made the universe,
And who sits enthroned above.

No doubt or fear will fill our hearts.
The perfect love of Christ the Lord
Will drive out all the worries.
We're promised in His word.

No hassles or injustice
Will be the things we see,
For we'll know the Judge of Glory
Is in control of you and me.

So, when we walk in heaven
As we sing and praise the King,
We'll notice some things missing,
But they won't be worth a thing.

GOD, YOU ARE

God of goodness, God of grace
My refuge and my hiding place.

God of righteousness divine
I am yours and you are mine.

God Most Holy, King of life
Savior in my time of strife.

God all knowing, God Most High
The one who hears me when I cry.

God of Heaven, God of Earth
Your love's granted me my worth.

God Redeemer, God unbound
All I need in you is found.

God of power, God of might
All the world's within your sight.

God eternal, God of time
I bask within your love sublime.

God Creator, God of truth
Praise and worship, all for you.

God the Father, God the Son
Holy Spirit, three in one.

HAND IN HAND IN HAND

A Christian marriage is based on
Abiding by God's word
For we, the Church, are the radiant bride
And the Bridegroom is the Lord.

And within each marriage union
We all must understand
The only way to make it work
Is to live hand in hand in hand.

Each partner holds the hand of
The one they truly love,
And with the hand that is not held
They hold the hand above.

For only when each partner
Is linked to God's own son
Can their marriage grow and prosper
Until their days are done.

HARVEST TIME

Lord, please harvest this life that you've given to me
So that when I wing heavenward, your dear face I'll see.

Take the sickle of righteousness and tackle the tares
Of the world that can trip me and try to ensnare.

Bundle them tight and throw them into the flames.
I ask this, dear Jesus, in your holy name.

Take the winnow of truth and let the chaff be no more.
Let the wind of your love, Lord, blow it right out the door.

For the chaff tries to lead me to give it first place
In my life; yet I know that I won't by your grace.

For no matter the bounty you give in this world
It's nothing compared to your love, blessed Lord.

So we thank you, dear Jesus, at this special time
For the harvest of fields and the harvest of lives.

HOPE, LIKE A CANDLE

Hope, like a candle, appears in dark days
To warm, and to lighten our faltering ways.
A faith in tomorrow and what it may bring
Of goodness and mercy from Jesus, our King.

Hope, like a candle, will glimmer and glow.
And to the whole world will forever show
The light of God's promise, His love and His care
For even in darkness, the Light shines out there.

Hope, like a candle, starts with just a spark
That grows into light that dispels all the dark.
We must ever be ready to defend our hope.
To tell how in life's darkness, it helps us to cope.

Hope, like a candle, can be quickly snuffed out.
We must cling close to Jesus and never let doubt
Allow us to think that our God cannot do
What is needed for rescue for me and for you.

I AM NEVER ALONE

*Because God has said, "Never will I leave
you; never will I forsake you."*

Hebrews 13:5 NIV

I know that I am not alone;
My Savior's always near
To love me and protect me,
To wipe away each tear.
There's not a second in each day
That He's not by my side.
My heart is Jesus' temple
Where the Holy Spirit resides.
God's peace is always on me;
I know His precious grace.
No time or distance can divide.
He'll find me in my place.
I know His grace and mercy.
I know his matchless love.
I know my Savior's watching
In heaven, up above.
I have the joy of being
In God's hand and I know
No matter where I walk on earth,
That I am not alone.

I CALL HIM

I call him Protector for all through my life
He has shown His protection in moments of strife.
My voice will eternally shout songs of praise
For my Jesus Protector, and His saving ways.

I call Him my Teacher, for His holy Word
Will show me the right way to live in this world.
I'll tell all I meet of the things that I've learned
That Jesus, my Teacher, taught me to discern.

I call Him my Brother, a glorious thing,
For now I am reborn, a child of the King.
I daily discuss in communion so sweet,
With Jesus, my Brother. Those times can't be beat!

I call him Advisor for in times of doubt
I go to His Word and then figure it out.
His answers don't always agree with my own
But Jesus, Advisor, His love has times shown.

I call Him whenever I need and He's there
To show that He loves me and He really cares.
But for now I will bring this poem to an end
And tell you, especially, I call Him my Friend.

I CAN'T DO THIS WITHOUT YOU

I can touch others with a servant's hand
And recognize their need.
But I can't do this without you-
This fact is true indeed.

I can hear sorrow in a stranger's voice
And lend a helping hand.
But I can't do this without you-
This fact I understand.

I can tell others of the great work of God,
With boldness, without fear.
But I can't do this without you-
I need you standing near.

I can be a true friend to all people
Who do not have a friend.
But I can't do this without you –
My need will never end.

I can lead souls to your marvelous throne
To receive your love, mercy and grace.
But I can't do this without you –
No other can take your place.

So, Lord, help me steadfastly stay every day
With my eyes focused only on you.
For I can't do this without you –
This fact I know is true.

I FEAR NO MORE

*In my anguish I cried to the LORD, and he
answered by setting me free. The LORD is with me;
I will not be afraid. What can man do to me"*

Psalm 118:5-6 NIV

When my troubles all besieged me,
And no end to them I'd see,
Then I cried out to the Lord,
And in love He set me free.

I know that when He's with me,
I will not be afraid.
I acknowledge all His power,
And my trust on Him is stayed.

And puny man can't hurt me,
Or cause me to despair
For I sit within the shelter
Of the Shepherd's loving care.

There is no throne or kingdom
That can over me prevail
If I will just abide in Him,
For my strength alone is frail.

Not time, nor place, nor circumstance
Can ever make be quake
For my Shepherd's told me in His word
That he never will forsake.

There's something I remember
And this one fact is very true,
That with my God beside me,
What can puny mankind do?

For man's slight power is fleeting,
But the Shepherd's power remains,
It's strong enough to bear the cross
To atone for mankind's stains.

And strong enough to change a life
When a sin-filled heart repents
And, in knowledge of God's greatest love,
To Calvary's cross it went.

It then received the grace and love
From heaven's treasure store
And can now proclaim for all to hear,
"With God, I fear no more!".

I KNOW

I'm secure in the knowledge. I need know one thing:
That I'm loved by my God; I'm a child of the king.

I know that whenever I find myself lost
That He'll come and find me, no matter the cost.

I know that His love will forever be mine
If I but abide in His great love divine.

I know that He loves me, and no matter the sin,
He'll be quick to forgive me, if I confess it to Him.

I know that His love will all times pass the test
And God's will for my life will be e'er for my best.

I know that no matter where I travel and roam
That's He's right there beside me; I'm never alone.

I know that this sounds like too good to be true,
But the same thing's a free gift, availed now to you.

You just have to give God a repentant heart
And your life of abundance will that moment start.

Abundance not of the world's kind of style
But abundance in God's love, and that is worthwhile.

A life filled with peace, joy, and mercy and grace
If you will bring your life and on the cross place

Your sorrows, and troubles, your pain and despair
You'll meet the great Savior on Calvary there.

And then in a voice that is humble and mild,
He'll say, "Welcome home, now, for you are my child".

I NEVER WALK ALONE

The Lord and I are walking;
We're friends along life's path.
I know He'll never leave me.
I know His love will last.

I know that He's my Savior;
I stand upon the Rock.
I know that I'll reach heaven
When there's no time on life's clock.

I know that I can access
His power and His might,
No matter what the circumstance,
No matter day or night.

I know, without my Savior,
No joy would my life bring.
But, with the Savior by my side,
I can achieve all things.

There is no principality,
No throne, no king or man
Can stand and triumph o'er me,
For my King has a plan.

A life plan that was started
When I yielded up my life
To the Christ who died on Calv'ry,
Amidst the pain and strife.

I know the world will see me
As one that's not the same
As those who live a carnal life
And don't know Jesus' name.

But if I stand up for my Lord
And daily walk His way,
I do not need to fear the words
That Satan's folk will say.

I know that God created me;
With love He knit my frame.
I am the Savior's masterpiece,
And no other is the same.

So, with my heart full of God's love,
His peace and joy are mine.
I can have sweet communion
With my Savior, so divine.

I await the time I'll be called home
To trod the streets of gold
And shout from mansion's rooftop
That I never walked alone.

I WAS NOT BOUGHT WITH PRECIOUS GOLD

For you know that it was not with perishable things
such as silver or gold that you were redeemed
from the empty way of life handed down to you
from your forefathers, but with the precious blood
of Christ, a lamb without blemish or defect.

1 Peter 1:18-19 NIV

I gave up all the empty ways
Passed down to me in sin,
And gained salvation for my soul
When Jesus took me in.

I was not bought with precious gold;
No silver paid my worth.
I was redeemed by Jesus Christ
And His sacrifice on earth.

His flesh was torn and bleeding;
His precious blood was shed.
He wore the crown of cruel thorns
Upon His holy head.

Christ, the sacrificial Lamb,
With no blemish, mark or stain,
Took on Himself the sins of all
And on the cross remained.

He could have called his angels,
But he hung there, oh so still,
When he called "It is finished",
God's plan was then fulfilled.

And when they put Him in the tomb,
The world thought they'd won
And gloried in the gruesome death
Of God's own precious Son.

But they were not around the tomb
In that resurrection hour
When Christ arose and conquered death
In God's redeeming power.

For now he sits in heaven
At the Holy Father's right
And intercedes for sin-stained man
With power and with might.

I will be ever thankful
That my ransom was not paid
With gold or gems or silver,
For their value would not stay.

But with the blood of Christ, the Lamb,
My salvation is secured,
And quiet assurance fills my heart.
This fact I know is sure.

Eternity is mine now,
And when I leave this place
I know that I will walk in heaven
And see Jesus, face to face.

I'll ever praise His holy name,
And bow before His throne
And praise the day His blood redeemed,
And he claimed me as His own.

I WILL NOT BE SHAKEN

*I have set the LORD always before me. Because
he is at my right hand, I will not be shaken.*

I have set the LORD before me; He's here at my right side.
No circumstance can shake me if I, in God, abide.

I'll listen to His precepts and walk His narrow way.
No circumstance can shake me if I, in God, will stay.

But Satan will not like that and he will try to break
The bond I have with my God, and try to make me shake.

But with the LORD beside me, with His great strength and power,
I can withstand the evil one, in each minute of each hour.

The LORD will not forsake me; I know He'll not depart.
The only thing I have to do is give my God my heart.

He'll place the sin-stained heart I bring in the shadow of the cross
And death will be defeated, and the grave will suffer loss.

For when I slip these earthly bounds and stand at heaven's door,
I know my joy-filled soul will sing, "I'm here for evermore."

I know that all my earthly time will fade and fall away
And, with the throng who've gone before, I'll sing God's holy praise.

In days to come in glory, when the heavenly roll is taken,
I'll say, "My God was always at my side, and I would not be shaken."

I WILL STAND UPON THE MOUNTAIN

I will stand upon the mountain
And sing my Savior's praise.
I will tell all of His righteousness
And all His holy ways.

I will stand upon the mountain
And tell to all the lost
That my Savior died on Calvary
And paid the pain-filled cost.

I will stand upon the mountain
And never will I cease
To tell the sin-stained people
Of God's amazing peace.

I will stand upon the mountain
And tell them of His grace,
His mercy and provision,
Until I've run the race.

Then I'll stand upon the mountain
Upon Zion's holy hill
And Christ will be there with me
In communion, quiet and still.

I'LL NEVER UNDERSTAND

Beyond the clouds, in heaven's realm,
You gladly left your place
To come to earth as helpless babe
To ransom Adam's race.

You did not need to leave that place
At God the Father's hand.
Why would a king leave glory bright?
I'll never understand.

And yet you came to earth to save
All mankind from his sin
So heaven's gate would open wide
And all your saints go in.

While here on earth, you strove to show
God's great redemption plan
That made a bridge from God himself
To all of sin-stained man.

And those who choose to bend the knee
Whose mouth said, "You are Lord."
Will spend eternal times in heaven
And praise in one accord.

So, thank you, Lord, for helping me
From sin to come unbound,
And knowing that, no matter what,
My hope in you is found.

I'M BLESSED

I'm blessed. I'm so blessed by the love God has shown.
He never forsakes me. I am never alone.
He's with me in valleys and on mountain tops high.
He hears me and holds me whenever I cry.

I'm blessed. I'm so blessed by the mercy He's given
He reached down and placed me on the pathway to Heaven.
He took what I offered, a repentant heart,
And said to me, "Now, child, I will never depart."

I'm blessed. I'm so blessed by His grace and his plan
That created a bridge between Himself and man.
He sent Jesus Christ down to earth as a babe
That all hearts that will hear and submit will be saved.

I am blessed by the fact that he loves me, no doubt,
And I know that with my God I will ne'er be without
His love and His mercy, provision and care.
I know that my God will always be there.

Just yield all your past and your present times too
And God will be faithful and give life to you -
A life full of blessings and then you can say
"I'm blessed. I'm so blessed 'cause I chose God's right way".

IN THE MORNING

*But I will sing of your strength, in the morning
I will sing of your love; for you are my
fortress, my refuge in times of trouble.*

Psalm 59:16 NIV

In each new morning, when the day is brand new,
When your blessings are freshly made known
I will sing of your power, might and great strength
As they all are so handily shown.
I will sing of your love that's so gracious and free,
Of your mercy and grace and much more.
You loved me so much that you died on the cross.
I am ransomed, redeemed and restored.
And you are my fortress in moments of fear,
To you, Lord, can I run in distress.
I can bring my petitions before your throne
And, in love, you choose this child to bless.
I brought you my heart full of sin and despair,
When I fell at your feet at the cross,
You said, "Come, my child, and never more leave.
I died because you're worth the cost.
But in my Father's power, and in His great plan,
I wrested the power from the grave.
So that all who will call on the name of the Lord
From eternal damnation I'll save."
So, I thank you, dear Jesus, for all that you've done
And for all that you're going to do.
I will sing of your mercy, your grace, and your love
In the morning, when the day is brand new.

IS YOUR NAME ON THE KING'S MONEY?

Is your name on the King's money?
Did you give it up in love?
Do you know that this investment
Will pay dividends above?

When the King piles high your givings
And then tabulates your due,
Will your pile be in relation
To what God bestowed on you?

Will He know that you have given
All you could, in sacrifice,
Knowing that lost souls were rescued
From the Devil's own device?

Or will He see you gave Him
Only what was second-best?
Will He know you gave a pittance
While you hoarded all the rest?

And so, my friend, be mindful
When you give unto the King.
When you give Him all you have now
He will give you everything.

When you enter into heaven
And the other saints you join,
You'll be pleased when Jesus draws near
And shows your name upon His coin.

KYROS MOMENTS

Lord, give me a *kyros* moment
When I come to know your power.
When the way my heart perceives you
Becomes clearer by the hour.

Lord, give me a *kyros* moment
A time of great import
When all I knew will fall away
In the light of your Good Word.

Lord, give me a *kyros* moment
When significance is given
To your death and resurrection
That made man's path to heaven.

Lord, give me a *kyros* moment
And let me fill it with all praise
That you alone are worthy of.
Help me appreciate your grace.

Kyros: A moment of time in which something special happens

LETTER TO MY FATHER

This is just a quick note to say thanks for all that you have done and what I know you will continue to do for me, your daughter. Words cannot ever fully express what you mean to me.

First of all, I would like to thank you for your love. Even if everyone else in the world would turn against me, I know that your love would be a constant in my life. There is no time when I could not call for help, knowing that you would do your best for me. There is no place I could ever go where your love would not be there with me. Thanks for loving me.

Then, I would like to thank you for the grace and mercy that you have always extended to me. In the times when I really messed up and thought that you could never forgive me, you reached out your loving hands, turned my face towards you, and I always heard you say," I forgive you, because I love you." You have showed me mercy on several occasions, and I just wanted to say what a difference that has made in my life.

I would also like to thank you for the many situations in my life that I thought were unbearable, and yet you made sure that I experienced them so that I would grow. When I tried and failed, you were there to give words of encouragement, and when I succeeded, you were there to share my triumph. I couldn't be the woman I am today without those experiences!

Lastly, I would like to thank you for my earthly father. Although he had his human frailties, he too was a man of great love and compassion. I have experienced his grace and mercy on more than one occasion. I always knew that he loved me, even at the times when I was most unlovable. He loved me because I was his daughter, but mostly because he first loved you.

So, thanks for all that you have given me and done for me. I know that one day I will join you and my earthly father in heaven, and together my dad and I will praise you together forever.

I love you,
Your daughter

LIFE'S HARVEST

The farmer was seated down in his chair
And viewed God's bounty that he saw there.
The turkey sat upon the plate
And all the food he saw looked great.
Outside, the barns were filled with hay
Enough to last him many a day.
The harvest of the garden canned
And winter wood was stacked at hand.
"The Lord's been good", the farmer thought.
"He's blessed me with all that I sought"
He leaned far back upon his seat
And said "The harvest's now complete".
But then a thought came to his mind
He realized that he'd been blind,
For while his fields were free from weeds
He could not say the same indeed.
For when he thought of what he'd done
To bring some souls to God's own son,
He felt ashamed and began to pray
And here's the words he commenced to say.
"Dear Lord, I know you paid the cost
To save my soul when I was lost,
And yet I've let the world come in.
I beg forgiveness for my sin.
Please take away the spiritual tares
That cause me pain and give me cares
Please bind them up and to the flame
Consign them, Lord, in your holy name.
With the sickle of righteousness cut down the sin
And afresh with you, Lord, I'll begin
To use the winnow of truth to blow away
All the chaff of life so it will not stay.
Everything that keeps us apart, O Lord,
As it says in the Bible, your holy word.
Will be gone from my life for evermore
And your love for me will be outpoured.

And I'll tell all others of my great Lord
And of the love that's written in His word.
And when my heart no longer beats
You'll say, "The harvest of your life's complete."

LOOKING AHEAD TO GLORY

When I leave this shell of a body
And head for the home I've not known,
I will join the great throng of others
To whom God's great mercy was shown.
A mercy that reached down from heaven
And rescued our sin-fated souls,
The blood of His Son washed the sin stain
That gave us new life, made us whole.
And when I arrive up in glory
I will walk upon streets made of gold.
I will sing to the One who had saved me
A song that will never grow old.
I will dance on the pin points of mountains
Surrounded by clouds of delight,
I will bask in the Son shine of heaven.
His glory will be ever bright.
I will live in a mansion of silver
And be given a body, all new.
I will walk in perfect communion
With my Lord, who has loved me so true.
He will whisper eternity's secrets,
And at last I will then understand,
Why the Son of the Father had chosen
To come to earth, die and save fallen man.
But my time here on earth is not finished,
There's a task that God wants me to do,
That's to tell to those I meet daily
Of God's love, so strong and so true.
Of God's love that can transform existence
From despair to a life filled with peace,
When a repentant heart begs forgiveness
And receives grace that will never cease.

LORD, KEEP MY HAND ON THE HANDLE

*Here I am! I stand at the door and knock; if
anyone hears my voice and opens the door, I will
come in and eat with him, and he with me.*

Revelation 3:20 NIV

Lord, keep my hand on the handle
Of the door on which you knock.
For when I do, you'll enter in.
We'll fellowship and talk.

Lord, keep my hand on the handle
For when I hear your voice
I'll open wide and let you in
For you are now my choice.

Lord, keep my hand on the handle
And let me close it neat
When in those times of quiet
We communion, long and sweet.

Lord, keep my hand on the handle
When the world calls loud and long
And help me keep the door shut tight
For to you this soul belongs.

For the door of my heart is bolted
To the things of the world and sin.
And I rest secure in my Savior's love
For that door He entered in.

MY MAKER, SAVIOR, KING

You formed me 'neath my mother's heart
And loved me from the very start.
And I know that you'll ne'er depart
My maker, savior, king.

You know the hairs upon my head
You are the Prince, the Living Bread.
And by your hand, I'll e'er be led.
My maker, savior, king

Each thing I do, each thing I say
Will honor you is what I pray
I'll walk your straight and narrow way,
My maker, savior, king.

You paid the debt that I should claim.
You heard them sneer your holy name.
My life will never be the same,
My maker, savior, king.

When you reached down and took my hand
You rescued me from Satan's band.
And took my feet from sinking sand,
My maker, savior, king.

My heart and mind belong to you.
And to your ways I will be true
You'll help me with all that I do,
My maker, savior, king.

NO MATTER WHERE

O LORD God Almighty, who is like you? You are mighty,
O LORD, and your faithfulness surrounds you.

Psalm 89:7-9 NIV

I stand upon the mountain peaks and view majestic span;
I then recall the valley times when we walked hand in hand.
When times were dark and light was scarce, I knew I would not fall,
For I was held within your grasp; you are my all in all.
I knew no king or power or throne would ever conquer me,
For if I have you, Lord, with me then that is all I need.
I stand upon the valley floor and recall mountain hours,
When I stood strong and without fear - I rested in your power.
I know you will sustain me, Lord, throughout my woes and strife.
I know you'll bring me through these times; I owe you all my life.
When the night is at its darkest and the moon cannot be seen,
I hold firm to my faith, dear Lord, for I know where we've been.
So, if I stand upon the peaks or on the valley floor,
I know that you will not forsake; I'm yours forevermore.
I'll know your love and peace and joy, your mercy and your grace.
I know you'll walk right by my side, no matter where the place.
No matter what the circumstance, no matter what the time,
I know I'll win the victor's crown – I'm yours and you are mine.

NO ROOM AT THE INN

No room at the inn for the one who created
This earth and all it contains.
No room at the inn for the one who can order
The wind, and the seas and the rains.

No room at the inn for the one who commanded
The earth to be born with one breath.
No room at the inn for the one who has fashioned
A home for each beast to have rest.

No room at the inn for the one who will yield up
His life without counting the cost.
No room at the inn for the one who will cover
The sins of the repentant lost.

There's room in my heart, Lord. Please enter and stay
As each day in your love I abide.
There's room for your mercy, your grace and your love.
As you, in my heart, now reside.

There's room for no other; you alone are my Lord.
No other can e'er take your place.
There's room for the blessing you daily provide;
I'm sustained by your mercy and grace.

There's room in my life for the lost that you show;
May I never refuse to be kind.
There's room up in heaven, where we'll walk hand in hand,
When I leave this flawed earth far behind.

ON THE ROAD HEADING HOME

With confidence, I can firmly say
Without a doubt, to you
That earth is not my home at all;
I'm only passing through.

And while I walk this earthly globe,
I know within my heart,
The Father's mercy, love and goodness
From me will not depart.

There is no place that I can hide
Without them coming by.
I'm continuously surrounded
No matter what I try.

And when it comes for me to go
And slip this poor flawed earth,
My soul will wing its way to heav'n
And there will find its worth.

And I will dwell in the Father's house,
A daughter of the King.
When I come to gates of heaven,
There's some things that I'll bring.

I'll bring the Father lofty praises
For all that He has done,
And a heart that has been ransomed
Through Jesus Christ, His son.

I'll bring remembrance of the times
His faithfulness was shown,
And gratitude for the precious hour
I was claimed as the Father's own.

There's also things I will not bring
To Glory on that day
Like fear and doubt and worry,
For they'll all have passed away.

For when I see my Savior's face,
My Redeemer King and Friend
I'll know that sweet communion,
And time will have no end.

Throughout all time eternal,
I'll sing praises to the Lamb
Who, when I yielded up my heart,
Received me as I am.

But loved me far too much to see me
Stay with sin-stained soul,
And used His blood on Calvary
To cleanse and make me whole.

He took my sins upon His back;
He did not count the cost
And gave to me His righteousness
For without it, I was lost.

So, as I walk here on this earth,
My focus has become
To the hour I'll walk in Glory,
And will know that I am home.

POEM OF THANKSGIVING

I thank you, Lord, for Calvary.
You saved my soul and set me free.
You took my debt and paid the price.
You've given me eternal life.

And though I know I can't repay
The price you paid, I yet can say
"I thank you, Lord, with all my might
For rescued soul and my new life."

PRESS ON TO THE PRIZE

*I press on toward the goal to win the prize for which
God has called me heavenward in Christ Jesus.*

Philippians 3:14 NIV

Although I cannot see the end, I run toward the line.
For each day helps me near the prize that Christ has said is mine.
And though I'll stumble, I won't fall; I'm held in God's own hand.
His strength is mine, His power too. This truth I understand.
I do not run the race alone, for as I round each bend,
I run with Christ right by my side – my Savior and my friend.
I do not know how long the race, but I know the Victor well.
My Lord and my Redeemer has run the race as well.
He too looked forward to the prize- the Father's own right hand.
And daily as He walked on earth, He spoke the Father's plan.
He did not shout his lineage as God's own precious son,
But humbly lived His life on earth, until His work was done.
The closer that I get each day will cause my heart to soar,
Each step I run will bring me close to heaven, evermore.
So, I will press on to the goal; the world won't stop my pace,
I know each step on life's long course is full of love and grace.
And when the finish line's in view, and my race is almost won,
I pray I'll hear the Father say, "Well done, my child, well done."

PSALM 2007

Oh, Great and Almighty God. You are an awesome God. Father of all who call on your name and the name of your son, Jesus Christ. Creator of the world that surrounds us. You are He who orders the wind to blow and directs where its power will be demonstrated, and the oceans ebb and flow at your bidding. The animals of the earth, the birds of the air and things that inhabit the depths of the seas live their lives to the rhythms and cycles that you have ordained. I am also your creation, and you are everything to me.

You are my friend. When friends who speak words of sweetness fall away and I seem to stand alone, I do <u>not</u> stand alone, for you are with me. Your Word says that you will never leave me or forsake me, and I trust the integrity of those words. There is no situation or circumstance where you would take your presence from me.

You are my protector. When the world devises wicked schemes to trap me and trip me up, you give me wings of the eagle to rise above the snares of the world and above my own selfish desires. When I rest in the shadow of your mighty arm, peace washes over me and I revel in your unfailing love. Peace is not the absence of danger in my life, but it is being in your presence.

You are my hope. Spending eternity with you and your son, Jesus Christ, is the prize at the end of the race I run each day. Victory lies in obeying your word, and living according to your directives. I look neither left nor right as I run the race, and focus on the rich reward awaiting me when I leave the confines and limitations of this earthly life and reach heaven, where you will be waiting for me.

You are my confidante. There is nothing I can tell you or think that you do not already know before the words leave my mouth or the idea formulates in my mind. And yet you wait until I walk up to your Throne of Grace with my petitions before giving me the answer that is always in my best interest, even though at times I cannot see that in my humanity. However, trusting you I push forward to do your will.

You have intimate knowledge of me. You gifted me with the gift of who I was when you fearfully and wonderfully crafted me beneath my mother's beating heart. You gift me now with who I am, as I walk your narrow way. And I know that you will gift me with who I will become, through all my earthly years, of which you alone know the number.

You give me a life of abundance, not as the world defines it, but a life full of your unconditional love and blessings. You have blessed me with family and friends, some who know you and some who don't. You have given me talents and abilities and have mandated that I use them to win the lost into your kingdom.

Oh, Great and Almighty God. You are an awesome God.

QUESTIONS AND ANSWERS

Why did you pick me to be your child?
Why rescue me from my sin?
Why make me whole from the inside out?
Why make my life clean within?
Why sacrifice your son on the cross?
Why did he take my place?
Why should you make me a child of the king?
Why show this sinner such grace?

How many times did you knock on my heart?
How many times I said no?
How many ways did you show me you cared?
How can a poor sinner know?
How can I thank you when words aren't enough?
How can I ever repay?
How can I show what your love means to me?
How can I show you each day?

I know that you love me, although I had sinned,
But you gave me your love and your grace
When I knelt down at Calvary and yielded my life
And acknowledged my heart's sin-filled place.
I know I will try to tell others each day
Of your mercy and grace and your love.
And I'll sing all your praises while down here on earth
And when my soul soars to heaven above.

REMEMBERANCE

*I cried out to God for help. I cried out to God to hear
me. When I was in distress, I sought the Lord.*

Psalm 27:1-2 NIV

I cried out to God for deliverance;
I prayed that my prayers He would hear.
In times of distress, I cried to the Lord
And I know that He saw all my tears.

And at night, when I prayed without ceasing
Then my soul just could not be eased,
For I thought that the Lord had rejected
All my heartfelt prayers and my pleas.

And I wondered if God had rejected
And if I'd know His favour once more.
Had His unfailing love up and vanished?
That thought hurt my heart to the core.

I wondered if He'd ever show mercy.
His compassion'd be withheld from me.
Then I thought to myself, "I will think on you, Lord,
And all of your marvelous deeds.

I will ponder your miracles of ages past
And what you have done all in might
And my soul will rejoice for all that you've done
And my thinking will clear and be right.

For Your ways, O my God, are holy.
What god is so great as my Lord?
You display all your power and all of your might
And your miracles are seen in the world.

Your mighty arm brought us redemption
The people that you chose and love.
And my soul soars to heaven with grateful thanks
When I remember all that you've done.

SAVED AND SECURE

I give them eternal life, and they shall never perish; no one can snatch them out of my hand. My Father, who has given them to me, is greater than all; no one can snatch them out of my Father's hand. I and the Father are one.

John 10:28-30 NIV

My children have eternal life,
And they shall never die.
No one can snatch them from my hand
For they are ever mine.

My Father, who gave them to me,
Is greater than all things -
All powers and principalities,
All armies and all kings.

They rest within my Father's hand,
For He and I are one.
And there they'll rest in peace and love
'Til time on earth is done.

When time comes to an end on earth,
Eternity is where
My children will abide with me,
And still rest in my care.

We'll walk and talk in glory land,
In that land beyond the sea.
For now, my children look ahead
As they rest secure in me.

SHEEP SAVED BY THE LAMB

But he was pierced for our transgressions, he was crushed for our iniquities; the punishment that brought us peace was upon him, and by his wounds we are healed. We all, like sheep, have gone astray, each of us has turned to his own way; and the LORD has laid on him the iniquity of us all.

Isaiah 53:5-6 NIV

We, like sheep, had gone astray.
Each had turned to his own way.
But our great God ordained a way-
The sheep would be saved by the Lamb.

All our hearts were stained with sin.
Through heaven's gates no entrance in.
But our great God gave us the win –
The sheep could be saved by the Lamb.

On Calv'ry's tree Christ hung and bled
With thorny crown upon His head.
Though sinless, he hung in my stead –
This sheep was saved by the Lamb.

He did not count the cost too high.
His blood did my redemption buy.
He knew from start He'd have to die
So the sheep could be saved by the Lamb.

So all the days I walk on earth
My soul now knows its heavenly worth.
I thank my God for second birth
When this sheep was saved by the Lamb.

So yield your heart to Christ today;
He is the Life, the Truth, the Way.
With peaceful heart, you can daily say
"I'm a sheep that was saved by the Lamb."

SIN'S AFTERMATH

Then the man and his wife heard the sound of
the Lord God as he was walking in the garden
in the cool of the day, and they hid from the
LORD God among the trees of the garden.

Genesis 3:8 NIV

Adam and Eve, in their guilt, fear and shame,
Hid from the LORD when He called out their name.
"Where are you, my children? Come out, now I say"
But Adam said, "No, Lord. We've no clothes. We're afraid."
Then God asked who'd told them their bodies were bare,
And asked if they'd eaten of the tree standing there.
"The woman you gave me, she gave me the fruit."
Adam said that the serpent had said it was good.
Then God asked the woman, "What is this you have done?
No tree was forbidden, excepting that one."
The woman then answered, "The serpent deceived.
He said I'd gain knowledge, and dear God, I believed."
God then told the serpent, "For the evil you've done
You'll be cursed, and forever, you will crawl on the ground.
And the offspring of woman, and the children of you
Will forever hold enmity for eternity through.
Your head will be crushed, and you'll strike at man's heel."
To the woman, God added, "Great birth pains you'll feel."
And the man was advised that the ground would be cursed,
And before any harvest, great toil would come first.
There'd be thorns. There'd be thistles, and sweat on man's brow,
And when man's life was over, he'd return to the ground.
Then God had compassion, and made garments of skin.
To cover their bodies, but could not cover their sin.
And because man now had knowledge of evil and good
He'd not be enabled to live long as he should.
So the couple was banished from Eden to toil
At earning their living by working the soil.

Then God, in his wisdom, had the angel stand guard.
Back and forth flashed the guardian's great flaming sword.
And Eden was closed. No more could man see
In the centre of Eden, the life-giving tree.

SOARING

I soar on the wind of your power alone
Secure in the mercy and love you have shown.

I know that you'll be there in my times of need.
To lift me and hold me, to guide me and lead.

And just when I think that I'll fall from the sky,
You lift me on your wings and then I can fly.

I thrill to the feel of the wind in my face
And marvel each day at the breadth of your grace.

Your love will sustain me; your Word told me so,
And I soar on the wind of your power alone.

SOMEONE ELSE'S SONG

The words like "death" and "suffering"
Rang loud upon my ear.
The music had a dirgeful sound
That I didn't want to hear.
The words spoke of a dieing Christ,
The savior of the world,
Who suffered crucifixion while,
At Him, snide words were hurled.
Again the words said lives were changed
When hearts repented true.
The King of Glory died for all –
But He arose in glory too.
I heard the words and melody
But the music all seemed wrong,
And then I came to realize
It was someone else's song.
I knew I had to make it mine,
So I yielded up my heart.
So all the words of my life song
Could have a brand new start.
I sing that song throughout the day.
I sing for all to hear.
There is no time that I can stop
And I sing it loud and clear.
The words now have a happy tune,
For now I have Christ's peace.
I have His grace and mercy
And love that will not cease.
The music has a happy lilt;
Discordant sounds not there.
For now I know I'll always rest
Within the Master's care.
I am now in God's family,
In a place where I belong
And now the words bring comfort;
They're not someone else's song.

SPLINTER IN MY HEART

I've got a splinter in my heart
That came from an old, rugged tree.
I don't ever want to pull it out;
It's a part of Calvary.

It's soaked in the blood of Jesus Christ
The blood that He shed for me –
The blood that ran from His hands, head and feet
As He hung there on Calvary.

And I know that there's power in that splinter
It can change life for you and me.
For Christ rose again, in triumph and might,
Mere days after dark Calvary.

This blood soaked and powerful splinter
Was placed there when, on bended knee,
I admitted my sin and became God's special child
And thanked Jesus for Calvary.

It only hurts me when I sin
And I cause God's pain to be keen
For He sent His Son to die on that cross
To save me at Calvary.

But I know if I only confess my sin
He'll forgive and restore unto me
All the peace and joy that are mine to claim
Because His Son died at Calvary.

THE 23RD PSALM REVISITED

The Lord is my Shepherd. I'll not know a need.
I know that my Savior will guide me and lead.

In green meadow pastures, He makes me to lie.
I know with my Savior my soul will not die.

Beside the still waters, He leads me in love.
I know that my Jesus is watching above.

His hand leads me gently for righteousness' sake.
I know my Redeemer will never forsake.

In the great name of Jesus, I walk righteousness' path.
I know that His favour on my life He'll cast.

Though I walk through the valley of death and despair,
I know that my Savior will walk with me there.

No evil can harm me; I belong to my God.
I'm comforted daily by His staff and His rod.

He prepares me a table though enemies near.
With my Christ beside me, I've nothing to fear.

On my head He pours oil, and my cup overflows.
By His grace and mercy, His great love He shows.

I know that His goodness and His loving ways
Will follow me throughout my God-numbered days.

In the house of the Lord, for eternity, I'll dwell
With the quiet assurance that He saved me from hell.

And I'll spend my time telling on this earth, while I'm here,
That the Lord is my Shepherd and I've nothing to fear.

THE ALTAR

My life was all in ruins,
In shambles at my feet;
The spring of joy had been dried up
And life was bittersweet.

I cried out to the Savior,
"Lord, what can I do now?
I want to fix my life, Lord,
But I just do not know how."

He did not speak a single word
But bent down at my feet,
And picked each stone of deep despair
And placed them true and neat.

He reached again and picked some stones
Of doubt and discontent
And placed them on the other stones.
I knew not what He meant.

And then more stones were added.
His movements never faltered.
And when I looked upon the Lord,
I saw He'd built an altar.

He'd taken all my ruined life,
Each broken shard and rubble,
And built an altar where I go
In times of joy and trouble.

His love holds all the stones in place.
I can return each day
And thank Him for His faithfulness
As I walk His narrow way.

THE BREAD AND LIVING WATER

Then Jesus declared, "I am the bread of life.
He who comes to me will never go hungry, and
he who believes in me will never be thirsty.

John 6:35 NIV

"I am the bread of life", He said. "All those who come to me
Will thirst and hunger never more, if they will just believe."
The world gets hungry for the things that do not satisfy,
And each new day, they'll thirst again until their souls are dry.
No matter how much they possess, they covet with their eyes
And try to fill the God-shaped void with things that money buys.
There'll come a day when everyone will fall upon their knees
And proclaim Christ as Lord of all when His great power they see.
And yet the ones who know Him now, and call upon His name
Are bold to swear allegiance, without fear and without shame.
He is our King Redeemer, our Savior and our Lord,
And all of us here on this earth feed daily on His Word.
It fills our souls without compare; we'll never thirst again.
For all the Living Water has washed away our sin.
We need this Living Water to cleanse and to refresh.
The Bread of Life will sustain us until our time to rest.
And when our soul wings upward and we enter heaven's door,
The Bread and Living Water will be ours forevermore.

THE LAMB BECAME MY SHEPHERD

Christ, the sacrificial Lamb,
Who was killed on Calvary's hill,
Went willingly to that torturous death
To fulfill His father's will.

He suffered as they pierced His limbs
And bore a thorny crown.
He could have called His angelic hordes
To lift His body down.

But, knowing that sin kept me
In bondage to Satan's power,
He hung, bruised and beaten, upon the cross
Until that final hour.

Then with His dieing breath, He asked
His holy father why
He had forsaken Christ that day.
Then He gave up his spirit and died.

But do not worry, and do not fret,
For Christ arose in power
And stole the victory from the grave
In that resurrection hour.

His foes were not around to see
His wonder and might revealed.
They all believed that they had won,
For the tomb's mouth had been sealed.

But stone could not stop Jesus Christ
From arising that third day
As He had said, when He walked this earth.
He's the truth, the life, the way!

And now He sits at God's right hand,
In heaven, whence He came.
Because of that resurrection day,
The world won't ever be the same.

For now we have a bridge that spans
From heaven to this earth.
And those that call on Jesus' name
Will be given second birth.

And Christ will keep and guide us,
For like sheep we go astray,
And the Lamb became my Shepherd,
On that resurrection day.

THE LAW OF CHRIST

When you see your brother burdened
By a heavy, heavy load,
When you see your sister fallen
On the shoulder of life's road,
When you see what lies just hidden
By a smile or glad face,
Then help them with their burden
Just as you've known God's grace.

When you hear the tears of mourning
And the cries of deep despair,
When you hear the sobs of sorrow
When a loved one does not care,
When you hear the sounds of anguish
When they hear the doctor's words,
Then just put your arms around them.
Do it as unto the Lord.

When you feel that deep injustice
Is a fact in someone's life,
When you feel that they are suffering
With conflict and with strife,
When you feel that what you can give
Is too little, then my words heed
And remember that with our God,
We can do just what we need.

For the power of our Savior
Is what we can call upon
To defend the rights of others
When the circumstance is wrong.
And the Holy Spirit will lead us
And will help to guide our way
So that to the world's lost people
Whom we meet, then we can say,

"My God loves you so much,
So just yield to Him your heart,
And His arms of love will hold you,
And from you He'll not depart.
You will find peace and contentment.
You will find a joy untold.
And He'll be your own Good Shepherd
When you come into the fold."

THE LIGHTHOUSE

The lighthouse shines its welcome beam
To all the ships at sea.
The darkness flees in that beam's path
And gives security.

The ships that sail into the light
Well know what that beam means,
Safe passage into waters deep
Led by that golden beam.

The Lighthouse also leads me home;
It's built firm upon the Rock.
And winds of trouble, strife and woe
Won't harm, destroy or knock.

My ship will reach the cove I seek;
No harm will it befall
For at the start of troubled winds
On Jesus' name I call.

He is the Lighthouse Keeper,
And always hears my plea.
I know He wants me safely home
Because He so loves me.

So, when the winds pick up and blow
And when my ship is tossed
On billowed sea, I know for sure
Without Him, I'd be lost.

The safety of my ship assured
I know is His great plan.
And nevermore will my ship sail
Without resting in His hand.

THE MAN WHO PERSEVERES

Blessed is the man who perseveres under trial, because when he has stood the test, he will receive the crown of life that God has promised to those who love him.

James 1:12 NIV

When tribulations come around,
Let Jesus calm your fears
For blessed is the man who perseveres.

No matter what conditions are
The reasons for your tears
There's naught can harm the man who perseveres.

For when he has withstood the test,
And stood strong throughout the years,
A crown's the reward for the man who perseveres.

The word of God has stated this,
In truth so plain and clear,
That the Lord will bless the man who perseveres.

THE MAN WITHOUT THE SPIRIT

*The man without the Spirit does not accept the
things that come from the Spirit of God, for they
are foolishness to him, and he cannot understand
them, because they are spiritually discerned.*

1 Corinthians 2:14 NIV

The man without the Spirit
Cannot accept the things,
The things of God – the knowledge
That the Holy Spirit brings.
He thinks that they are foolish
And cannot understand
The way that God created
His great salvation plan.
Without the Spirit's leading,
The lessons he won't learn
For all the holy things of God
Are spiritually discerned.
He will not ever fathom
How deep his need for God,
And that there is redemption
In Christ's death on the cross.
He will not know the mercy,
The grace and love bestowed.
The peace and joy of knowing Christ,
All this he will not know.
But, with the Spirit's leading,
He will be shown the truth –
That Jesus died for all mankind,
He died for me and you.
And when he brings his sin- filled life
And lays it at the cross
The sin will all be washed away,
But there will still be loss -

The loss of worry and of fear,
The guilt and all the shame,
Replaced with unsurpassing joy
And peace in Jesus' name.

THE QUILT

The quilter took the scrap of cloth
And stitched it to the base.
And then another scrap was set
Against the first one's place.
Each scrap had colour, not the same
Each one a different shape.
This process was repeated
Until the quilt was fully made.
Who would have thought such different scraps
Such beauty would display?
The quilt portrayed a grand design
With each scrap a part to play.
Each part did not within itself
Hold beauty in its heart.
But stitched by master hands, they went
From scraps to work of art.

My Master also takes the scraps
Of my life, and designs
A work of art that's seen by all-
His Master piece divine.
Each scrap is used, none go to waste,
From each a lesson learned.
Each one is different from the rest;
But each is placed in turn
And stitched together with His love
Until the work is done.
The sum of all the different scraps
Is greater than the one.
Without the Master's touch, I know
The scraps would never be
A thing of beauty, peace and joy
That all the world can see.

THE SOLDIERS

The soldiers mocked my Savior King;
A purple robe He wore.
They did not see His majesty,
So a thorny crown He bore.
They mockingly called out to Him,
"Hail, king of all the Jews!"
They struck with staffs and spit on Him;
He suffered their abuse.
He could have called angelic hordes
To save Him, yet he stayed
Because He knew the Father's plan –
It was the only way.
Then He was led away to go
To dark Golgotha's hill.
Again, He never used His power
And fulfilled His Father's will
To die a death so full of pain,
To ransom man from sin.
To be entombed for three long days
And then to rise again.
And, sometime after death, these soldiers
Came before Christ's throne
They each fell prostrate at His feet
And were judged for what they'd done.
Their thoughtless words and actions
Decided their own fate,
They all were cast into Hell's fire
To suffer torments great.
Although, in life, they bowed and paid
Their homage mockingly
In death, again their knees were bowed
As Christ's deity they'd see.
And, in their anguish, they would know
Who Christ was, and recall
That they had mocked and crucified
The Greatest One of All.

THERE IS A GOD!

The fool says in his heart, "There is no God." They are corrupt, their deeds are vile; there is no one who does good.

Psalm 14:1 NIV

A fool will shout to all the world
That God does not exist.
With no regard to what he sees,
At God he shakes his fist.

It would but take a glance around
To see that God is real,
For just one look at what He's done
His power would reveal.

The mountains stretch up to the clouds.
The birds all fly on high.
The tiny ant will work and hoard,
When winter's coming nigh.

A baby's born into this world -
A true miracle, I know,
And there's a wonder when you see
Each finger and each nose.

They are corrupt; their deeds are vile.
Fools choose not to see Him there.
But I know that my God exists
For I rest within His care.

I see the wonders He has done
Within my life and out.
"There is a God," I shout aloud,
"Of this there is no doubt."

THINK ON THESE THINGS

*Finally, brothers, whatever is true, whatever is noble,
whatever is right, whatever is pure, whatever is lovely,
whatever is admirable—if anything is excellent
or praiseworthy—think about such things.*

Philippians 4:8 NIV

Whatever is noble,
Whatever is right –
Think on all these things,
Both day and night.

Whatever is lovely,
Whatever is pure –
Think on all these things,
And your walk will be sure.

Whatever is excellent
And worthy of praise –
Think on all these things
Throughout all your days.

Whatever is admirable,
Written down in God's word –
Think on these things
For it pleases the Lord.

Whatever is honest,
And whatever is true
Thinking on these things
Will edify you.

WHAT ANGELS CANNOT KNOW

The angels know the face of God.
They bow before His throne.
But there's one thing they cannot know -
God's power in sins atoned.

They cannot know the peace that fills
A true repentant heart.
They cannot know the pure, pure joy
God's new-found love imparts.

They cannot know a life renewed –
The gift of second birth.
That gift's reserved for people who
Give up the things of earth.

The cannot know the death to self
God's children ever know.
They cannot know the sense of joy
When God's mercy is bestowed.

They cannot know the gratitude
That swells within the soul
Of one whose life was washed anew
In the blood that made them whole.

But I know all these things from God
His love and mercy shown,
His awesome power in my life
And all my sins atoned.

WHEN

When I'm partaking of the bread
I do recall you hung and bled
And took my sins upon your head.
I thank you, Lord.

When I'm partaking of the wine
I know that all the sins were mine
And yet you left your home divine.
I thank you, Lord.

When I take part in needed prayer,
I somehow sense your presence there.
This shows me just how much you care.
I thank you, Lord.

And when my life is filled with doubt
I know that you will work it out
And then I'll raise a joyous shout
To thank you, Lord.